# A Rookie Comes to Town

Sandy Heitmeier Thompson

**Artwork by Toby Mikle**

ISBN 979-8-88644-146-8 (Paperback)
ISBN 979-8-88644-148-2 (Hardcover)
ISBN 979-8-88644-147-5 (Digital)


First Edition



Covenant Books
11661 Hwy 707
Murrells Inlet, SC 29576
www.covenantbooks.com

## To My Friends

You warm me with your presence
We share memories of our past
We cheer and console each other
That's why our friendships last.

We chit—chat and share secrets
We keep each other in our prayers
We strive to be honest and loyal
We know each other cares.

Friends are precious gifts
That can't be bought or sold
So, you see my dear companions
Our bond is pure gold!

Anish and his family were new in town. They had left India because the company Anish's parents worked for had asked if they would help open a new office in the United States. The Patels thought it over and decided it would be a wonderful experience for their family, so they accepted the company's offer.

It was Labor Day, which is in September. The sun was shining brightly, and the weather was warm and dry. Mrs. Patel decided to take advantage of some local sales and went shopping for items that could be used for their new home. Mr. Patel took Anish to the zoo. They enjoyed observing the animals. As they walked through the zoo, Anish noticed several recreation areas with kids playing. Anish spoke English very well, but he was a little shy about joining in with the other children.

As they approached the restaurants located in the middle of the zoo, Mr. Patel's cell phone began ringing. "This is work," Mr. Patel informed his son. "Please stay in this area while I take this call."

Anish found a comfortable-looking bench, sat down, and simply took in his surroundings. This area of the park was very pretty; it had large trees and plenty of chirping and chattering birds. The birds jockeyed for opportunities to pick up food dropped by human visitors. Their sounds and movements brought a smile to Anish's face.

As Anish watched the birds scramble for food, he felt something feathery brush up against his ankles. He looked down and saw some coins on the ground. Before he could reach down and pick them up to examine them, a pigeon darted out from underneath the bench, grabbed the coins, and jumped up on the seat next to him.

Anish laughed and said, “Wow! A bird that collects coins.”

Surprisingly, he heard a reply: "That's why they call me Cash, young man."

Anish introduced himself to the pigeon and told him that he recently moved to the area. The young boy then asked, "Where do you keep your stash of cash?"

"I have a secret place. Maybe one day I will show you when I know I can trust you. I am cautious because there is a certain squirrel that often watches me. I think that furry creature wants to steal my loot," explained Cash.

"Well, do you ever spend any of your currency?" questioned the curious young boy.

"I'm very thrifty," the bird responded, "but I will make an investment if I think it is worthwhile. In fact, I have some human friends around your age who showed me how to purchase one of those ancestry kits so that I could find out more about my heritage. I will introduce you to my pals so you can become friends too."

“That would be awesome! By the way, did you find out anything interesting about your background?” inquired Anish.

“I sure did!” Cash replied with great enthusiasm. “I found out that I am a descendant of a famous female homing pigeon named Cher Ami. That means ‘dear friend’ in French.

"Homing pigeons are particularly good at remembering where they live and finding their way back home, even when they've been transported tremendous distances away from it. Sometimes these pigeons are used to carry important messages. These are called carrier pigeons.

"Cher Ami was one of many carrier pigeons used by the US Army during World War I. But Cher Ami's story is extra special.

"A battalion of American soldiers was lost and surrounded by unfriendly forces. They were out of food and ammunition. They needed to contact their allies to get help, but their phones didn't work. Carrier pigeons were their only hope of getting a message to friendly forces.

"One by one, the carrier pigeons took off with paper messages inside small canisters tied to their legs. And one by one, the pigeons were shot down by the unfriendly soldiers.

"Cher Ami was the last pigeon. As Cher Ami rose from the brush to fly, enemy soldiers saw her and opened fire, wounding her. Cher Ami went down but managed to get back up and continue flying. She arrived at her loft in the Army headquarters twenty-five miles away in just twenty-five minutes, helping to save the lives of almost two hundred American soldiers.

"Cher Ami had been shot through the breast and blinded in one eye, and she had a leg hanging on by only a tendon. Army medics worked to save her life. They were unable to save her leg, so they carved a small wooden one for her. She was even awarded a medal."

Anish exclaimed, "Wow! She truly was a hero!"

"Yes, she was. I'm very proud that I am related to her," Cash responded. "Now, how about you, Anish? Is tomorrow your first day of school?"

"Yes, it is. I'm excited and a little frightened at the same time because everything is new to me," admitted Anish.

“Hmm. I have an idea of how to introduce you to my human friends. Can you meet me at the sports field next to the school tomorrow when class lets out?” asked Cash.

“Sure. I’ll check with my parents first to make sure it’s okay. We live right behind the field, so they will be able to watch me from our backyard if they want,” responded Anish.

Anish was at school bright and early on Tuesday. The teachers and students were very nice to the newcomer and welcomed him as a member of the student body. It was certainly an interesting day at school for Anish, but he could not wait to meet Cash at the sports field once class let out.

The school bell rang, and the anxious lad made his way to the field, which had been set up for soccer, with goals at each end and the soccer field marked off with chalk.

Anish was standing on the sidelines looking for Cash when four kids approached. One said, "Hello. Are you Anish?"

"Yes, I am," said the smiling boy.

"Hi. I'm Brett. And this is my brother, Blake, and our friends, Gavin and Maya," said the blond-haired lad.

Just then, Cash, who was wearing a sports cap and had a whistle hanging from his neck, rolled a soccer ball onto the field with his beak. "I see you've met our new friend," he stated.

"There is a soccer tournament Saturday, and I thought the five of you might want to join the competition. Do you think that is something you would like to do?" asked the pigeon.

All the kids agreed that this was a great idea.

“Wow, Cash. That is a brand-new ball. Where did you get it?” asked Blake, wondering.

“I bought it with some of my money. I think this is a good investment. I thought you could train with it after school this week,” suggested Coach Cash.

Anish told the group that he had never played soccer before, even though the sport is very popular in India, so his new friends would have to teach him how to play.

Maya began describing the game. “The object of the game is to get the soccer ball into the opposing team’s goal,” she explained. “Whoever scores the most goals wins the game. A team normally scores a goal by moving the ball down the field, which is done by passing the ball to each other to get in a good position to kick the ball into the goal. Players cannot use their hands to move the ball, except for the goalies who defend their goals.”

Brett added, "The most important thing is for us to play as a team, make smart passes to each other, and get in position to score a goal."

Blake showed Anish a push kick, or an "inside-of-the-foot kick," which is used for short, accurate passing.

Gavin demonstrated an instep kick, which uses the upper surface of the foot, also referred to as "the laces." This kick is mainly used for shooting at the goal.

"What's a good name for our team?" asked Cash.

"How about the *Flying Pigeons*," Maya suggested. The kids all concurred.

Coach Cash had the team practice passing the ball to each other as they moved down the field toward the other team's goal.

Anish was a great teammate. He listened very well, worked hard to learn the different kinds of kicks, and unselfishly passed the ball to his teammates.

To end the practice, Coach Cash put the ball on the ground and huddled the team around it.

As the teammates formed a circle, a squirrel dashed into the huddle, jumped on top of the ball, juggled some coins, and chanted out loud, "Look what I found, and now they are mine." Then it jumped off the ball and zipped away as fast as it had come.

Although bewildered by the squirrel, Coach Cash was determined to keep his team focused. "Great practice, team. We'll meet here at the same time tomorrow."

"But, Coach, aren't you worried about your coins?" asked Blake.

Cash calmly responded, "We'll deal with that swindler after the tournament. Let's just concentrate on soccer until then."

During practice on Wednesday, Coach Cash called for a water break and put down his whistle. Unexpectedly, the squirrel ran onto the field, swiped the whistle, and dropped a coin on the ground. As the little bushy-tailed thief scampered away, it chuckled and yelled out, “That’s my payment for my new whistle.”

Each day, the team had a great practice. And each day, the squirrel played a prank on Coach Cash.

On Thursday, the squirrel snatched Cash's hat and left a coin.

On Friday, the squirrel stole Cash's clipboard with his coaching notes and left another coin.

The tournament started early Saturday morning. Many spectators were gathered around the field, some of them standing and others sitting on foldable chairs, to cheer for their favorite teams. There were several brackets of teams based on the ages of the players. For this tournament, each team had five players instead of the normal eleven to allow more kids to play. Each game was one period of fifteen minutes. If a team lost a game, they were eliminated from the tournament.

The Flying Pigeons' age group had two brackets with four teams each.

The Flying Pigeons needed to win three straight games to win the tournament for their age group.

Game 1 for the Pigeons was a high-scoring game. Brett, Gavin, Maya, and Blake each scored a goal. And Anish made some terrific passes to set them up. The Flying Pigeons won their first game 6 to 5.

Following the same script as the first game, game 2 for the Pigeons was also a high-scoring game. The team did a great job of moving the ball down the field, and for most of the goals, Anish was the one making key passes to get his teammates in position to score their goals. The Flying Pigeons won 4 to 3.

As the team waited to play the championship game, Coach Cash huddled with the team for some coaching instructions.

“Okay, Pigeons,” he said, “we are playing some good soccer, but we need to change our strategy for the next game. We are playing the *Rhinos*. They are really good at scoring goals and defending their goal. Our strategy will be to play a tough defense and focus on stopping them from scoring. We’ll be patient and wait for our best opportunity to try to score,” explained Coach Cash.

Both teams were super-excited when the Pigeons kicked off to start the game. The teams went back and forth up and down the field. The pace of the game was furious; both teams were very quick and played amazing defense. The game became even more intense as the game clock ticked down.

With thirty seconds left in the game, one of the Rhinos broke out and headed toward the Pigeons' goal. It looked like the Rhinos were about to score when, like a bolt of lightning, Anish swooped in to steal the ball and passed it to Gavin before he tripped and fell to the ground face-first. Although in pain, Anish thought of the bravery of Cher Ami and found the strength to get back up to finish the game.

The Rhinos surrounded Gavin, but he was able to get off an instep kick down the field.

It was a stampede as both teams raced down the field to get the ball. All the while, the clock kept ticking.

Out of the crowd of players emerged Anish, racing ahead of the rest. He got to the ball first and made a perfect kick to send the ball into the goal. The Flying Pigeons won the game 1 to 0.

Anish was so excited that, after the game, he threw the soccer ball high in the air, hitting a tree branch. Out of the tree dropped a cloth bag filled with coins, a hat, a whistle, and a clipboard.

As the unhappy squirrel watched from the tree, Cash picked up the bag and exclaimed, "What a game! What a team! What a finish!"

# About the Author

Years ago, a devasting hurricane hit the city where Sandy Thompson lived. Residents evacuated, scattering all across the country. Houses were destroyed, and companies moved to other states. The many uprooted people had to start over. Their children had to leave their friends and attend new schools.

Mrs. Thompson maintained close relationships with many of her former students and their families. Parents often called to tell her what their children were doing in their new schools. Sandy remembers one touching story about a school that established a "buddy bench" on its playground. New students or those who had no one to play with could sit on this special bench to alert their peers, who were encouraged to ask those on the bench to join them. Sandy thought this was such a wonderful strategy for helping kids meet one another and form friendships.

Years later, Sandy described this special bench to some of her lifelong friends. They laughed, imagining what it would be like for them to meet on such a bench today. They certainly would not come to the bench to join a game of tag, but perhaps they would exchange recipes or tell one another about their aches and pains. Sandy realized how long she has been friends with so many wonderful people. Though many now live far away, they remain a big part of her life, and Sandy smiles whenever she contemplates how lucky she is.

www.ingramcontent.com/pod-product-compliance
Ingram Content Group UK Ltd.
Pitfield, Milton Keynes, MK11 3LW, UK
UKHW061955290726
14090UKWH00021B/1245

9 798886 441468